AN ALARM HAND OF THE CLOCK

MANAS AGRAWAL

ISBN 979-8-89277-933-3

Dedication

To all the lazy geniuses all over the world.

Set Your Alarms

Introduction

After the hour hand, minute hand and second hand, here comes our very old fourth hand of the clock: the alarm hand. It is a wake-up call for all of us to brush up on our old philosophies and see the broader picture of life in a new way. Set your alarms now and get ready to awaken in a new world with:

Meditation

Living Your Dreams

Shaping Your Destiny

Searching for Happiness

And so on...

An Alarm Hand of the Clock awakens, arises and inspires you to be unstoppable until you reach your goal in its own way. It inculcates in you a rational approach towards life, shaping your personality into a mature figure through intellectual and social intelligence. By giving you the technique of controlling your emotions, it prevents you from getting carried away by others or personal sentiments, allowing you to make decisions in your life with common sense.

Meditation

Being yourself without knowing yourself can give rise to misconceptions about yourself. So first and foremost, know yourself, then be yourself.

Judge yourself by observing what type of questions you ask yourself. Someone else's queries will merely be an adventure for you, but only your questions will delve deep inside you. Reflect daily on yourself, and gradually you will dispel doubts about your existence. If you don't, there will be no one else to work on you dedicatedly.

A personality with a confused mindset can't leave a positive impact on a progressive society. They have to be sure about who they are; only then can they provide vision to others. Otherwise, being themselves can merely manifest as an egotistical nature because if they are uncertain about themselves, they cannot form a concrete self-image, which society needs.

Meditate more and you will find yourself closer. By being closer to yourself, you will feel that slowly and steadily, you are gaining control over yourself. Upon discovering your strengths, practice them relentlessly until you achieve mastery.

Every generation has visionaries like Socrates, Plato, Aristotle, Confucius, etc. So why wait and look for others to be your guide? So this time, why not the guide be...YOU?

Live Your Dreams

Most of the time, when a man marries a woman of the same profession, they expect their child to choose the same occupation they are pursuing. However, in doing so, parents often block their children's creativity, which is essential for sound development. The core element of education is to develop thinking power, and if the thought process of choosing a vocation is pre-determined, the child may not reach the heights their parents expect. Although it may be tough for a growing child to choose the right career because every moment is new to them; it's not a matter of fear. One bold decision to pursue a career of their choice will teach them to stand on their own for the rest of their life; otherwise, they may become dependent personalities in every aspect of life.

Allow your children to create their own unbiased destiny. Their creativity will then make them symbols of whatever the system is later on.

Live your dreams, neither those of your parents nor of anonymous.

Shape Your Destiny

Control your emotions, and you will be able to control yourself. When you control yourself, you will not be controlled by others. Then, you will be able to control what you want from yourself.

When you realise that you are getting things done on your terms and conditions, you will find that others will help you and facilitate getting things done for you.

Whenever you achieve success, you are just entering from the old system to a new one with new responsibilities. Before that, people often calculate many things about it. Emotions form such a vivid picture that they start to make you worry or create anxiety about things that don't even exist in the new scenario. They portray things, giving you a feeling of closeness to your designed structure, and making the image larger than life. However, if you are aware of the thin difference between your creativity and reality, you won't get carried away by others' or personal sentiments.

Basics always remain the same. You can't escape daily routine necessities like waking up in the morning, freshening up, eating food, going to school or the office, etc. Whatever you do, your energy is consumed in that activity. Where your energy is utilised, your time is spent doing it. And where your time is invested, your destiny begins to take shape accordingly.

Your destiny is in your hands.

Google Search Happiness

When happy moments come, we see that they quickly slip away, and when we are in sad moments, they take a lot of time to pass. In happy times, we pray a lot, hoping that the second hand of the clock will move slowly, but our prayers hardly seem to work. Conversely, in sad times, we urge fervently for time to move swiftly.

However, neither the force of prayers nor the force of urgency seems to work at those times. So, in feeding anxieties to our innocent act of trying to control time, we forget that both joy and sorrow are in our hands. The steps we take in our lives, and the way we execute them determine the worth of our moments. If that precious event we were resisting against time for has gone, more happy moments can still be created. We can enjoy time with new friends over fresh gossip, appreciate the offered cup of tea from our wives/moms, engage ourselves in new activities like playing tombola, and visit temples and offer thanks to God for our good family and sound health. The size and taste of happiness may not be the same as that precious resisting moment for which we were urging the 'Lord Time', but these are also types of happiness, providing different feelings and tastes. When these feelings make us feel happy, then we realise that we are neither lacking in occasions for happiness nor do we have to rely on others for our happiness. Others can become part of our happiness too, but if we are alone, the choice is totally in our hands.

Happiness dwells in the heart of the seeker. It is also a law of nature; what we search for in this universe, we receive back from it.

Gentle Professional Animal

When we talk to each other, we get to know each other. In knowing each other, we get closer to each other. While closing, our expectations from the other rise, and in expecting, we get to know the likes and dislikes of others. In getting too personal, by mistake, we do the post-mortem of one another, and in that, we get to know their daily routine habits. Each one has different tastes, and when their tastes differ from ours, we find uncommonness in them from us. This sense of uncommonness creates distance when we find a habit with which we are uncomfortable or dislike. Disliking leads to hatred. Hatred separates us, leading to enmity with those whom we are closer to.

The more we take personally, the more poorly we manage. While getting biased towards someone, we become unfair to the other. It's better to keep our intent at some distance and shift our focus from people to our goal. Stop doing a thesis on them by reading their faces or body language; instead, invest your energy in finding your strengths.

Human terms are volatile; they need to be solidified occasionally at some social events or by throwing a party, and we should not rely on them. What is concrete is our aim, our work, which makes our presence worthwhile. Earn respect not by pleasing others but by becoming useful in your workplace.

Formal terms give rise to common sense, and friendly terms give rise to affective sense. So don't be affected by the presence of others, no matter how close they may be, making you non-judgemental rather than a sensible personality. Just have cordial terms with each one, making you part of society. But now you are grown-up and have to mature, so wherever you invest your energy, that work becomes the profession by which you are going to be known. If you are inducing your energy into making people happy, you will be known as a comedian. If you are involving yourself in playing games for your country, you will be rewarded as a sportsperson in that game, like a cricketer, swimmer, tennis player, etc. By pleasing people with your writing, you will be known as a writer, by singing as a singer, by dancing as a dancer, by teaching as a teacher, by engineering as an engineer, and so on. Whatever you do, in whichever sense you take a taste, finally, that inclination becomes your profession. Since we all are working for the development of society, we were tagged as social animals, but by fate or choice, we all are professional animals.

Gravity

A man without ethics is a man without gravity. Your knowledge may reach up to the sky, but your moral values are the ones that hold your feet to the ground. Without knowledge, you are a fool, but without ethics, you are an emotional fool.

Knowledge + Morality = Gravity

Your gravity dwells not only in taking your profession seriously but also in how much value you give to your parents, teachers, friends, elders and distant family members—whomever you know in your life. Only then will you be the owner of a sound personality, having a balanced mind and feeling more meaningful to yourself and to society.

On considering two types of intelligences:

1. Intelligence Quotient (IQ)
2. Emotional Intelligence (EI) or Emotional Quotient (EQ)

With IQ, you win the minds of high intellectuals, but with EI or EQ, you win the hearts of sentimental individuals. If you have knowledge but your ways are loud, your appearance will become abrasive, and if your ways are very pleasing but you don't have knowledge, you can't make space among academics/scholars.

IQ says – "Books are our best friends" but,

EQ says – "Love is Friendship."

With books, you may be left alone, but friends are the ones who never make you feel lonely. No matter how much knowledge you may hold, without the presence of others, you are nothing; your gravity remains uncalculated.

Lastly, if you live just to serve your stomach only, you will be regarded as a man, but if you have the aim of serving your society too, you will be remembered as an eminent man, a man of respect, a man of gravity.

Strings of Emotions

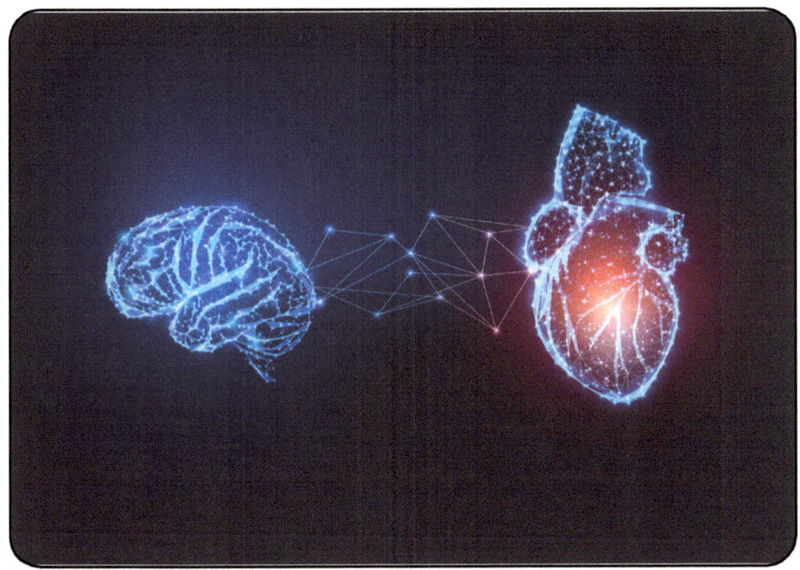

Behind every relationship, such as that of mom-son, son-dad, brother-sister, uncle-nephew, etc., there exist tendencies. By going vice versa, from the way of tendencies, relationships can be created even if you are not a blood relation to that individual. Circumstances and time play an important role in developing the same. Time is the most precious thing you can give to someone. When you give someone your personal time, they will feel that they are not just a pastime for you. They will feel very special about themselves. This feeling is magic in itself. And its magic is that in return, you get nicknames like cutie, sweetie, honey, baby, darling, etc., when you succeed in making space in the heart of the other.

A man can become emotionally balanced when he finds himself successful in stitching the net of emotions together with the surrounding elements in a fine way. When you are forming a bond with another, not only do you have to be fair to yourself, but you should also be very clear that you should not flirt with whom you are sharing emotional connectivity. The atmosphere of sentiments will then develop in the environment, and finally, the relationship thus gets named like brother, sister, uncle, aunt, etc., from the lustre of the heat of the knitted environment of feelings/emotions.

Mind Over Matter

What you practice will come in flow. No one can compel you to do something. And if you want to take control over yourself, you have to first practice your attitude alone. Thoughts shape our attitudes, and our manners when contemplated in solitude..

For getting a hold over oneself, people used to wear rings as a part of rituals/culture, but the astrologers won't reveal to you the science behind mannerisms. Instead, they charge heavy fees, making you their regular customer to take responsibility for your behavioural outcome.

The culture you practice at home will be exhibited in your attitude. The way you see or observe things in your daily life becomes your philosophy. If you think that wearing a ring of pearl can help you win over your anger, you are on the wrong track. You are thinking absurdly and making yourself a slave to the ring(s).

The delicate science behind anger is that the person on whom you are getting angry is not even slightly affected by your anger. Instead, you are harming your health, increasing your blood pressure and progressing towards major diseases like cancer.

Don't give your mind, body, heart and soul over to a small ring to have control over yourself. You can control your emotions when, in solitude, you understand the characteristics of these sentiments. All feelings are just a part of your creativity and nothing else. What matters is happiness and peace, for which all mankind is struggling. Then you can see yourself above all these emotions like greed, attachment, lust, etc. When you start seeing yourself above all the emotional creativities, you find that you are getting closer to yourself, and with mental strength, you can command over each and every sense.

Train your mind to hear your inner voice instead of getting distracted by others and supporting their arguments, for example, by wearing the stones suggested by unqualified astrologers. Your mind is with you 24x7; hence, work on it to assert yourself over every affecting entity surrounding you. What matters most is the state of mind in winning any battle(s) of life.

Author's Exceptional Works

INTUITION
PING! Hey! Listen. IT whispers softly.
PING! INTUITION, MY CHILD.
PING! MOM, WHO IS MY FATHER?
Necessity
Invention
MANAS AGRAWAL

www.ingramcontent.com/pod-product-compliance
Lightning Source LLC
LaVergne TN
LVHW021320160826
845679LV00001B/426

9798892779333